This Book Belongs To:

We hope you enjoy reading
Faithful Furry Friends: Service Dogs.

Written by The Sisters
Angela Pestello & Kathleen MacLeod

Illustrated by Alyssa May
Edited by John Gilbert
Copyright © 2020 Pig Pen Publishing LLC

ISBN: 978-1-7356323-0-8 (Hardcover)
ISBN: 978-1-7356323-1-5 (Paperback)
ISBN: 978-1-7356323-2-2 (Ebook)
Library of Congress Control Number: 2020915786

First printing edition 2020

Pig Pen Publishing LLC
PO Box 2772
Bentonville, AR 72712
www.pigpenpublishing.com

Hello! My name is Ranger. I'm a service dog. Have you ever seen a dog wearing a vest like mine? If so, then they are a service dog, too! We spend lots of time training to do special jobs that help people. We are very different than your dog at home. Service dogs are not pets.

My vest is very important. It's called a service vest, and it lets everyone know I'm at work. When I wear my vest, I can go almost anywhere with my owner. If you see a dog wearing a service vest, do not disturb them. Their vest means that they are paying attention to their job! I love my job, and if you pet me, I might get distracted. Never pet a service dog.

There are many types of service dogs. Some types of service dogs can be seizure alert, mobility support, police dogs, guide dogs and many more. To meet some of these dogs and learn what they do, you can read about them at the end of this book.

My friends and I start training when we are just 8 weeks old. Sometimes we live in a foster home for a year or more. Our foster families teach us how to be good puppies. Then we go to advanced training with amazing trainers. They teach us how to perform special tasks, so we can help people. Training is very hard and can take up to two years to complete!

Do you know what to do if a service dog with a vest comes up to you without their owner? Tell an adult right away! Service dogs are trained to go get help if their owner is in trouble.

Remember, if you see a service dog, like me, just look at them with your eyes. If you have questions, you can always ask the service dog's owner. They would be happy to talk to you about their dog and how they help them.

What did we learn:

- A service dog is not a pet.

- Service vests are important because they show when I am working.

- Do not pet a dog wearing a service vest.

- Service dogs spend years in training.

- If you see a service dog without their special person, tell an adult.

Guide Dog

Hi! My name is Poppy, and I am a guide dog. My job is to help Bree. She is blind and cannot see. My service vest has a handle for her to hold on to, so I can lead her from place to place. I'm trained to look both ways when crossing the street. I cross the road at crosswalks, find things like phones and keys, and even open elevators. I tell her when there is a step up or a step down. Bree depends on me to keep her safe.

Hearing Dog

Hello! My name is Max, and I am a hearing dog. I'm trained to help Casey because she is deaf. That means she can't hear. My job is to listen for doorbells, smoke alarms, alarm clocks, ringing phones, and much more. I nudge her with my nose or put my paw in her lap to get her attention. I am allowed to go everywhere with her as long as I wear my service vest!

Mobility Assistance Dog

My name is Scooter, and I'm a mobility assistance dog. My job is to help Dan navigate while using his wheelchair. I bring him the phone when it rings, open automatic doors, and pick things up if he drops them. I can even help Dan get up if he falls out of his wheelchair.

Diabetic Alert Dog

Hi! I'm Memphis. My sense of smell is so good that I can tell when somebody's blood sugar is too low or too high. My job is to help Walter, who has diabetes. I alert him by pawing or nudging him. I'm also trained to get help if Walter is too sick to care for himself.

Seizure Alert Dog

Hello! My name is Avery, and I am trained to find help if Katie is having a seizure. I can also alert her if she is about to have one. I lay down next to Katie to prevent injury while she's seizing. I know how to push a button that signals an alarm to notify others when she needs help. My job is to keep Katie safe!

Psychiatric Dog

I'm Chief, and I help Carlos. He suffers with PTSD from serving in the military. My friendship helps Carlos when he is sad or feeling nervous. I also remind him to take his medicine. When we are around a lot of people, I help Carlos feel safe and stay calm.

Autism Service Dog

My name is Bella. I help a little boy, Theo, who has autism. Sometimes he runs away and doesn't understand dangerous situations. I have been trained to be tethered to Theo. When we are tethered together, Theo cannot run away, and I protect him from harm. We spend a lot of time together, and I help Theo stay calm.

Allergy Dog

My name is Charlie, and my super sensitive nose has been trained to detect allergens. Braxton is my owner, and he is severely allergic to peanuts. With my help, he is able to avoid eating anything that might contain peanuts. When I smell peanuts, I make sure Braxton does not eat it. I go everywhere with Braxton, even to school.

Therapy Dog

Hi, my name is Rosie, and my job is to cheer people up when they are sad. I go any place where people need cheering up, like hospitals, nursing homes, and schools. I'm a therapy dog, which is different than a service dog. I am encouraged to interact with everyone. If you see me, you are allowed to pet and hug me all you want!

Military/Police Dog

I am Ranger, a police dog. I can sniff out drugs and bombs, or chase bad guys. I am trained to help find someone if they are lost, and I protect my partner from dangerous things. My vest is bullet proof. My job is to keep my partner and the community safe.